W9-BDK-715

STECK-VAUGHN

PAIR-IT BOOKS™

Cat Prints

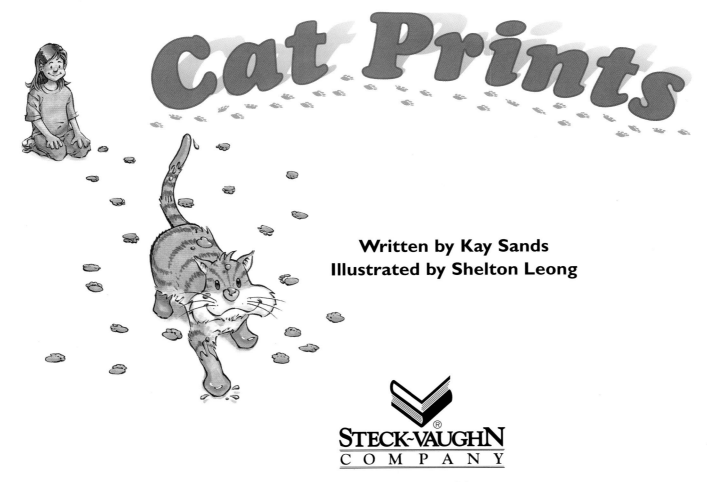

Written by Kay Sands
Illustrated by Shelton Leong

STECK-VAUGHN®
COMPANY

A Division of Harcourt Brace & Company

My cat runs

2

in the paint,

into the house,

across the rug,

up the stairs,

6

over the bed,

and into my arms.